WAYFARING

Praise for Tikuli's *Collection of Chaos* available from Leaky Boot Press

Tikuli's full blooded new book of poetry *Collection of Chaos* is too good to be missed. Her poems are direct and strong and I would not want to be on the wrong end of one of them. But when the occasion demands her writing is heartbreakingly tender and you'll want to put your arms around her.

John Lyle (Canadian singer-songwriter)

Collection of Chaos is the perfect title for Tikuli's impressive collection of poems. Dealing subjects as varied as human condition womanhood, nature, hope and loss – to name a few – each poem rings true with experience and thought. A new bright voice in Indian poetry, Tikuli proves that we have much to expect from this horizon, not to mention a lot to learn. *Collection of Chaos* is thus not only a fantastic collection, but also an important one, as it places life back where it lies, in the heart of chaos.

Sebastian Doubinsky (author, editor, academic)

The poetry in *Collection of Chaos* must be read. For those who enjoy structural unconventionality in poetry coupled with bold issues usually made invisible, this book offers a most mature poetry. For those who like it lyrical and light, the verses on nature will leave a permanent impression on your minds. And for some others who like to take it slow, to read a poem a day, know that each poem of this book is like a world in itself – offering you thoughts to think and maybe ideas to pen even. I got mine!

Sakshi Nanda (journalist/book critic, columnist, editor and blogger)

WAYFARING

a new collection of poems by
Tikuli

LEAKY BOOT PRESS

Wayfaring
by Tikuli

First published in 2017 by
Leaky Boot Press
http://www.leakyboot.com

Copyright © 2017 Tikuli
All rights reserved

No part of this book may be reproduced or transmitted in any form or by any means, electronic, mechanical, photocopying, recording, or otherwise, without prior written permission of the author.

ISBN: 978-1-909849-54-9

Contents

Dedication	9
Acknowledgements	11
Introduction	13

TRAINS

Winter	17
Snow	18
Rain	19
Mist	20
City Metro	21
The Local Train	22

EXILE POEMS

Homeland Memories	27
Bazaar	28
Exile	29
Winter	31
Ghosts of War	33
The Child Widow	35
Home	36
Entr'acte	37
My Mother: a prose poem	39

REMEMBRANCE

Grief	43
Dust	44
Haunted	45
Silence: a prose poem	46

Entr'acte	47
Sadness	48
Quietude	49
Us	50
Void	51
Parting	52
Reminiscence	54
Unrequited Love	56
Ephemeral	57
Scent	58
Quiet	59
Hush	60
Haunted	61
Floe	62
Absent	63
Words	64
Traces	65
Lost	66
Monsoon	67
Stones & Pebbles	68
Veiled	69
Parting	70
The Wait	71
Absence	72
Needs	73
Estrangement	74

TRAVEL

Solitude	77
Waiting	78
Trail	79
Echo	80
Kinnaur Revisited: a prose poem	81
The German Bakery—Bhagsunag	82
Rhanikhet	84
House	85
Wait	86
Drought	88

On the Banks of the Ganges	89
Ruins	91
The Last Meal	93

MOSAIC

Empty Is Full	97
Poetry This Month is Hexed	98
Lost Poems	99
Daydream	100
Illusions	101
Melancholia is…	102
Troubled Seasons	104
Scent	105
Exhaustion—1	106
Exhaustion—2	107
Exhaustion—3	109
Break-Up	110
Pause	111
Nocturne	112

ACROSTICS

Journey	115
Silhouette	116
River-Song	117
Phantasm	118
Topography	119
Funeral Pyre	120

DELHI POEMS

Hazrat Nizamuddin Auliya Dargah	123
Lodi Garden	125
Purple Rain: a prose poem	127
Medical Migrants	128
Scent of a Season	130
Summer, Noon in Delhi: a prose poem	131
Fever	132
The Lake	133
Black and White	134

Dedication

To friends, lovers, dreamers, wanderers and storytellers

This collection is dedicated to all those with a student heart. Forever learning is the only way to go. Thank you Kris Saknussemm for the wisdom, love and friendship that is deeper than anything I could have dreamed of. You are the finest teacher and friend anyone could ever have.

Nabina Das and Ritu Lalit, thank you for that gentle nudge to follow my dreams, unafraid and with confidence. You opened a whole new world to me.

I would like to thank James Goddard, publisher and editor at Leaky Boot Press. He imparted much counsel and advice, with a great deal of encouragement to me all through my writing journey and especially for this book.

Acknowledgements

Many of these poems were first published in various online journals *Dissident Voice, Le Zaparougue, MiCROW 8, The Smoking Book* (Poets Wear Prada Press, US), *Life and Legends, Levure Littéraire 10, The Enchanting Verses Literary Review, Open Road Review, Cafe Dissensus, Mnemosyne Literary Journal, The Criterion, Peregrine Muse, Knot Magazine, Asian Signature Magazine, TEKSTO, Peacock Journal, The Thumb Print—A Magazine From the East, Learning and Creativity Magazine,* Tuck *Magazine,* etc. Most have been revised for publication in this book.

Introduction

Poetry helped me change an old order. My chaotic and restrictive life made me turn to writing as a therapy. Many of my poems are intensely personal and at times I use nature or some other element as a mask to write about private feelings but mostly all my work is about 'laying bare'. It is about vulnerability. I learned to balance my energy meridians so sometimes an exhilarating moment or a frustrating one became a muse.

I had to deal with an inner critic too but I was open to learning and found good mentors and encouraging friends who supported my desire to write. Over the time this urge to pour out my angst began to recede and a new affair with words began. It challenged me to break barriers.

A snippet of overheard conversation, a sentence or phrase in a book, a piece of music, an interesting or unusual fact, a conversation with someone, the changing landscape while I travelled in and outside the city, became an inspiration. Poetry flushed out feelings, emotions, thoughts, questions that I never knew lay buried inside me.

My debut poetry book, *Collection Of Chaos* was published by Leaky Boot Press, England, in 2014. Most of the poems in this collection are very personal and drawn from my life experiences such as my concern for women's rights; my experience of unsatisfactory and troubled marriage; the love for my children and the difficulties we all face in everyday life.

Whereas, the poems in this new book, *Wayfaring,* go beyond just being elegiac, there is experiment of form, an interweaving of shapes, smells and the changing moods of a city where I grew up, an evocation of landscape, rural places, the rivers, mountains and forests. These poems have history and landscape running through their veins. There is also a form of protest which is a reflection of me and my convictions.

TRAINS

Winter

The sky was stained the blue of berries
on that peppery winter noon,
when we sat on the wooden bench,
outside the tea shop overlooking the valley,
we watched the toy train trundle slowly past
the oaks, rhododendrons, firs and pines
the hot masala chai melts our inner strife
filling us with a warm comfort

Snow

The narrow gauge waits in shadow,
a silhouette in grey winter light,
a poem uncoiling into oblivion,
in the near silence of falling snow
I listen for a heartbeat no longer there,
the soundlessness too strong for me,
just like the tea from the old tea shop

Rain

The edge of the rain slices the ruddy sun
with delicate knife like precision,
and turns one side of the valley grey,
on the sunlit side the shivering green
tries to cling to the fading light,
the wind snores, shifts, snarls,
rain-filled clouds clamber upwards
towards the mountain peaks,
in the valley, whistling its old song
a train crawls through the dappled grey

Mist

a wayward brushstroke
on a spring-like pallet
the little mountain train
is homeward bound
along the wandering waters
past the flaming rhododendrons
into the valley of yellow and gold
then a little town, pastel painted
tumbling down the forested hill
there and gone again
lost in the mountain's mist
and the steam from my tea

City Metro

laden with shopping bags
this poem rides the rush hour tide
at the metro station.
coffee in hand, a packet of sugar
gripped between its teeth,
a bag strapped across its chest,
hair escaping from a floral bandana,
talking into a bluetooth headset,
it makes its way to the waiting train,
leaving behind sillage of memory

The Local Train

in the stuffy train compartment
a woman reaches into her blouse
seeking the money hidden there,
she glares at the man opposite her
who watches staring, hoping
a little boy gazes through the window
his eyes fill with innocent wonder
as he stares at the unfolding world
his sister, with mischief in her eyes,
twirls her braided hair, over her lips,
beneath her nose, like a moustache,
two women, with their noisy kids,
inch their way through the crowd,
find an empty seat and settle there,
wedged together like orange segments,
the train darkens as it enters a tunnel
and a teenager's face is illuminated
in the light from his mobile phone,
against the shoulder of his companion,
who is staring at his own reflection
staring back at him from the outside,
a man dozes, another man, elderly,
in a red shirt, adjusts his reading glasses
and loses himself in a newspaper,
a woman closes the novel she is reading,
her thumb carefully marking the page,
she smiles, her amusement a private thing,

a laptop bag hanging from his shoulder,
a man in a suit, abuses into his iphone,
then hastily lowers his voice
and continues to pour out his anger,
in contrast, outside the window,
a dry, bleak lifelessness prevails,
the hellish summer sun spits fire,
devouring all life on earth,
bare trees, barren fields, small towns,
each glimpsed and then gone.
the music of the wheels goes on—
clickety-clack, click, clickety-clack.

EXILE POEMS

Homeland Memories

years ago I bid adieu to my homeland
autumn colours that stained my heart
have faded and the rivers that ran deep
in the lines of my hands have dried
that land is a distant dream, its ending
lost like a forgotten fragrance

sometimes restless nights are sheened
by light from the winter moon I watched
leaning from the window of the bus I took,
the cool air awakens distant memories,
as I travel back to my past, a village
nestled between mountains and streams

there I run shoeless in fields of saffron
chasing an invisible kite, the fiery chinar
warms my heart, silhouettes of walnut trees
spread their arms in welcome
outside our home you await my return
but as I reach out to you, you fade away

you are gone, like summer light at evening
it's been years since I last saw your face
maybe one day, when you see the moon
reflecting in the quiet waters of the lake
and hear a boatman's song echo in the breeze
I will be home never to leave you again

Bazaar

the spice shop perfumes the morning
in the streets of the old-city bazaar
as people hurry on private errands
a bangle seller displays his wares
promising good fortune to those who buy
at the tea stalls, people share stories
over a cup of hot masala chai
barefoot children chase imaginary kites
oblivious to the bustling crowd
a cow sits contemplating life
beset by flies it blinks its soulful eyes
women bargain with the grocers
for rice and lentils to feed hungry mouths
amidst traffic chaos people jostle for space
the afternoon sun drifts towards evening
strings of lights twinkle like fireflies
laughter and singing echo everywhere
flavours and aromas fill the night
and the city—like a new bride—
sashays dreamlike until the sun rises again

Exile

the sky that final evening
was smeared red with death,
and a tangible odour of fear
hung oppressively in the air,
by the half-shut windows

blood had petrified in my veins
mother moved about the rooms
disturbing the unnatural quiet,
the few things we still owned
were in neat bundles by the door

slowly, on his arthritic limbs,
baba mapped the contours of home
he absorbed the fading colours,
let memories settle on his skin
as fragile as a fine layer of dust

in a corner grandma sat quietly
huddled with her kangri,
her gaze lost in a different world
the children had long forgotten time
and surrendered to exhaustion

from my place near the window,
I envied their restive slumber,
as I watched our landscapes of pain,
between somewhere and nowhere,
the wail of an ambulance sounded

gunshots echoed through the air,
choked on dust and soot and pain
we waited, as the day became ash
then we passed quietly into the night,
towards a cold, unfamiliar sky

Winter

In the stillness of the old house
my fingers leave traces
on the dust-shrouded sepias of broken lives—
their names only half remembered—

parents, grandparents, siblings, cousins—
in the courtyard of our ancestral home,
surrounded by vast areas of snow
that now weigh heavy on my heart

as I close my eyes and find a dream
in which the mist of old memories
veil the far distant hills
the grey of sorrow clouds the sky

bare trees that stand transfixed
like freshly bleached skeletons,
their summer songs exorcised,
are stark sentinels of winter

I recall a bright wood fire blazing
fragrant with the scent of my homeland
children making figures like themselves
to celebrate the coming of new snow

but that was before innocence was lost
and the snow turned red with blood
as their sculptures gradually died
and vanished from sight forever

in the years since I last saw snow fall
winter has become a grisly metaphor
for the loss of life and hope
and things that will never be again

Ghosts of War

I see him, I see him
standing there, a body trapped in soul,
always watching
the rubble and memories of our home.

They'd found him
slumped by the bombed, ruined mosque,
his spectacles askew
on his shattered nose, his bloodied face,
his forearms crushed,
his white robe ragged and mud caked.

They'd dumped him
into a two-wheeled cart used for rubbish
and dragged him
to where he now stands in the picture
that a stranger sent
"your father" was scribbled on the back.

This was a reminder
of when the city smouldered under clouds
of dust and smoke,
when I was deafened by shrieking sirens
and the wails of
devastated lives—women and children.

The day when we,
my mother and I, forced by my father,
my beloved father,

braved the crowded and blood-stained road
to another land,
never again to return to our homeland.

The Child Widow

Exhausted,
the sun dropped into the river,
vermillion flowed with the water
before being wiped away by night
hunched over she sat at its bank,
tired, like a wilted flower,
her tonsured head shone
like the august moon,
slowly she rose to her feet,
a white shadow in the twilight,
and walked noiselessly away,
leaving behind the shards
of her broken childhood,
hunched over she sat at its bank,
tired, like a wilted flower,
her tonsured head shone
like the august moon,
slowly she rose to her feet,
a white shadow in the twilight,
and walked noiselessly away,
leaving behind the shards
of her broken childhood

Home

he often spoke of his home
his village house and hearth
the birdsong from the back yard
the old Neem tree's shadow
marking the passing of time

the hot summer afternoons
children lazing by the lily pond
the vapour trail graffiti on the sky—
while he wrote his love poems
beneath the laburnum's shade

eyes closed he breathed deeply
the scent of blossoms and earth
that reminded him of things left
in that silent haunted house
with its wayward stream behind

sometimes he could hear the echo
of his mother's slow footsteps
as she moved from room to room
fixing & making the house ready
expecting the always harsh winter

winter's coldness stayed in his heart
until spring came with its promise
of warmth and better days ahead
his journey home was long, so long
but the path to the village was clear

Entr'acte

the white wall of our house
absorbs the old apple tree's shadow
turning it into a shifting wonder
the sun drips from our tin roof
your bicycle rests below fiery chinars

in the kitchen a stove burns
on the table an old copper samovar
the lingering aroma of kahwa
translucent sugar, local breads, pickles
raisins and walnuts, all wait

two low wooden stools, a bench
copperware gleaming in the sun
half burnt incense on a silver plate
in a nearby room, tapestry cushions
rugs, kangris and hand woven shawls

photographs of us posing, silverware
a curio cabinet, on it a cigarette case
neatly arranged on the dressing table
silver jewellery, a comb, a kohl stick
and a walnut box waiting to be filled

jasmine floats in a crystal bowl
next to the bed, a neatly folded quilt
a pair of slippers on the floor,
musty books ramshackle on shelves
on the wall hang a calendar, a notepad

on the rose and green shaded porch,
a paddle loom dressed for work
on the steps I wait, as I do every day—
my belly swollen, a lotus bud in my hair—
for your return to make this house a home

My Mother: a prose poem

He sat beside me silent as a breath, wrapped in the wet, crumpled tissue memories of that summer, lay on his lap, his wrinkled hand resting on his walking stick. Then he spoke:

Your mother's hands were brown and soft just like the phulkas she made, she was an earth woman. I often closed my eyes when she sang, her songs rose from the soft rhythm of the water wheel, the tinkling of bells around the bullock's neck, the sweetness of the mustard flowers, and the crackle of the wood fire in her stove, they carried with them the scent of damp earth.

Often I would quietly slip in and listen to her sing as she went about doing her daily chores, her wet hair rolled in a towel or loosely tied in a bun with one or two loose strands framing her face.

It was a cruel summer that year, the river had dried and the cattle knelt and bowed their parched heads to the river bed pleading for a tickle of life, of life, the fields turned brown and the leafless trees stood naked and exposed as if atoning for their unknown sins under the merciless sky.

It was on such a summer day I found her hanging from the cross-beam, the wood was old and rot riddled but it held her weight well enough. Her hair, shorn off, lay in a jumbled pile on the floor, next to it were the clothes she had worn, the milk on the clay stove had boiled over and dried, the milk bottle smashed against the wall, the house smelled of rage, lust and struggles. In the courtyard, the clothesline had collapsed under the weight of sorrow, the swing lay dismantled and chained, a lone witness to her shame. The makeshift hammock hung limply from the tree, a kind neighbour had whisked you away as the town burned. Clasping your infant body like a broken doll and a picture of your mother in my pocket, I took refuge at a patchwork of shelters that had sprouted on the smouldering land a few of us sat under a small covering of rags, tarpaulin and sheet metal, holding whatever was left of our precious belongings.

Somewhere, a man sharpened the knife on a stone, click clack, click clack, the blade glistened in the dark, another one sang, his low mournful voice made the night bleed with absence and loss, but the sun rose just as it always did bearing no sense of loss, and with it, we too rose carrying our wounded identities to slip away into the folds of anonymity.

A few days ago, I walked through that part of the town where I lived and loved, where she sang her songs, our old haunts, the old well, our ancestral home, nothing lives there anymore, even the ghosts have moved on, but the river now flows to the brim and in the fields the mustard flowers bloom in abundance.

The earth, they say, still sings the songs of estrangement in memory of that summer and then the sky pours.

REMEMBRANCE

Grief

I see you in the slant of light
that streams in from a distant time,
your body translucent as the sea,
the river holds your face in watery hands,
your voice shivers on bare stones,
sand echoes your songs, your eyes,
emptied of seasons, gaze at me,
wrapping me in a quiet embrace,
filling themselves with my longings,
my heart, hollowed of words,
weighs heavy with the moments
I did not live with you,
I reach out for you through the mist,
but you withdraw in silence.

Dust

Night shivers on quiet trees,
the silver disc of midnight moon,
torn by the branches of conifers,
drags its light over rustling deodars,
drops behind houses at the valley's edge,
the cold air bears the fragrance
of tobacco smoke and timeworn wood,
silence and regret haunt me
as in me I feel your absence growing
like moss on the walls of our empty home,
when a shadow wavers I think it is you,
but I know you never come here now,
nightly, I move among memories,
hoping to feel your presence,
and when time rolls up the night,
like a well used prayer mat,
I return to my final resting place
carrying the dust of our dreams.

Haunted

She was like that empty house upon the hill
the silent, uneasy house where no one ever goes,
where scarred walls hold dark secrets
and windows are like empty eye sockets;
where there always seems to be movement,
the sound of a door closing, footsteps
a flicker of light in the emptiness—
haunted and haunting at the same time.

Silence: a prose poem

We were sitting by the river where we'd met a few days before.

There is a deathly silence today, he said,

"'Deathly' is the wrong word for silence. Death is not silent. It is more vociferous than life and anyway there is never complete silence, the mind is continuously moving through the quiet of the inanimate."

That's rubbish. Silent as the dead is a known idiom, he replied.

"It is, so is the quote, 'silence speaks louder than words.'"

Have you ever been to a cemetery, a morgue—or better still a graveyard, or stood 'quietly' where the dead are put to flames? You must. The noise of the dry bones overrides everything.

There is nothing louder than dead air, a dead relationship, dead dreams, dead promises. Death, my friend, is anything but silent." I paused.

Death may not be silent but silence can still be deathly and that's what I said, he insisted, though I felt his conviction wavering a little.

"Silence is not just lack of movement or sound. It is the same with death."

Entr'acte

Rain pours like old jazz,
scribbles itself onto roads
shimmering like piano keys,
liquid notes cling to trees,
a train leaves the station,
packed with salt laced bodies,
as night absorbs the evening

Sadness

when memories bleed
across silent waters
my thoughts turn to you
I glide backwards in time
like a phantom barge
on a somnolent river
of autumnal sadness
taking in everything
never filled—just fading
darkness agrees with me
from endlessness to endlessness,
we are finally as one

Quietude

rain falls in a tumble
of words, lines, poems
and then it stops.
Hope and grief slide
down the windowpanes,
I listen to the voices
filling spaces in the trees,
moonlight scythes the sky,
the river, grey and glass-cold,
glistens in quiet light
like a dream during sleep,
your body grows heavier
as I hold you in my arms
the day was a raging sea,
now it's as still as your breath

Us

in the luminous womb of rain drops
stories are told, repeated, forgotten,
then told again as if for the first time,
the songs you softly whistled
in our quiet togetherness,
dreams shuffled to dust,
a life unlived,
sun drenched in liquid green,
kitchen smokes and laughter,
a winter sky, flawlessly blue,
things unspeakable and unspoken,
a kitchen knife,
stained with the graffiti of infidelity,
two silhouettes that once were us

Void

loneliness curls in the spaces
between the notes of the rain,
the night bleeds neon,
reflects in puddles on the sidewalks,
cigarettes float like corpses
bloated with memories,
voices, tense with longing,
rustle through the trees,
possessed and restless
the midnight lingers

Parting

it isn't really hard to part
it is returning memories
like piercing like shards
that are so difficult to let go
unended conversations
the lost fragrances
nestled in my heart's void
places that are familiar—

coffee shops, hotel rooms,
bars, old notes in my diary
hunger not satisfied
words frozen in mid-air
crumpled pieces of paper
filled with unreadable words
the memory of your kisses
these are hard to let go

the constant abandoning
and the indifference
the obscure silences
a noose about my neck
wherever I go

whatever I do
whoever I am with
a sense of abandonment

infects everything
familiar and unfamiliar
when I look in a mirror
I see it in my eyes
looking back at me
the same abandonment
I saw in your eyes
when we last kissed

before the distance
between us stretched
into the distance
between universes

Reminiscence

Reminiscing, I roam the paths with him,
my loss hangs heavy in the air,
the landscape as parched as my heart,
you a shadow, a ghost, a dream unfulfilled.

Sometimes I hear you… soft whispers
riffled by the warm summer breeze,
your smile lights a dew drop,
I catch your scent from the fragrant trees.

Aromas of food and sleep are in the air
the house is flushed with warmth.
in my loneliness I call your name,
feel your misty breath on my face.

Your face is reflected in the window
you call out, but I don't hear…
my face is in the raindrops of your tears,
you live in me… it's you I know.

My body holds the shadows of your love,
you are no more, you left me all alone,
my body a graffiti of your fingerprints,
like those you left on everything you touched.

Time is just the blur of your shadow.
I won't forget you, I won't forget you…
or the soft tread of your feet
or your music echoing in my dreams.

Long years have passed since you left,
my sorrow failed to become songs of love,
the invisible remained invisible…
I miss you… I miss you… first love of my life.

Unrequited Love

She watched the red streak of the moon
trail over the lake and disappear... never to return,
leaving behind a looming shadow on the tainted waters.

Unrequited love is an orphan of silence, abandoned
to fend for itself, during the endless days
and never-ending nights.

Ephemeral

There is still a hint of autumn
in the breeze—fragile as a whisper
a quiet reminder of something fleeting

Scent

The winter breeze through the window,
a spider dangling on a single strand of silk,
thin branches trembling and weeping
but you, on such winter days
are the scent of lemongrass
not wanting to leave the teapot.

Quiet

Still heart
Empty nest
Bare branch

In the quiet,
things I forgot to say,
rustle in the wind

Hush

I lost you over time.
We had so much to say but nothing was said.
Mail stopped coming, online chats ceased.
Phone conversations became impersonal words,
between silences that we struggled to break.
Your laughter was forced,
you were always elsewhere, even when with me,
memories of our meeting began to fade,
until you became insubstantial mirage.
You tossed what we shared into the waves,
as you crossed the ocean between us.
Our brief encounter became an imaginary sojourn.
I didn't know any better,
I was in love with a lover I had imagined.
Now, you're only a faded painting on lonely afternoons,
a monochrome photograph during my solitary nights.

Haunted

Days that are as uncertain as you,
and nights that don't set me free,
each haunted by the other,
my life just a monochrome shadow,
caught in between,
such is the summer of your absence.

Floe

every tale of love,
imaginary or otherwise
is a non-stop parting of ways,
a floe, forever drifting
between what was
and what could have been.

Absent

the scent will slowly fade
like the last notes
of your favourite song,
ebbing into silence.

Words

bound by the sorrow of the unspoken
and the silence of the spoken words,
our hearts, are made of different stones.

Traces

my shadow lies quartered on the sidewalk
bleeding ink from its fault lines
everything is gone
except the traces of you inside me
immortalized in words

Lost

I grieve
for those parts of our lives
which you buried
while they were still pulsating
with life

Monsoon

It is that time of the year
when the evenings smell like a breakup
and it is impossible to look at the things
without sniffing the heartbreak in the air

Stones & Pebbles

I sit on the ancient rocks
gazing at the evening sky bleeding
onto the bare breast of the ocean
a cloud catches fire and turns to ash
merging with the deepening blue
deep shadows consume everything
I open my fist and watch
the stones sink to the ocean bed
finally home.

Veiled

At the threshold of summer
I stand
still locked in the melancholy
of winter
An invisible poem
imprisoned in prose

Parting

We became strangers that night.
A brief encounter
when you colonized my body
in the hotel room
charged with the smell of sex.
It was a prelude
to the harsh winters ahead
and all the coming seasons
lost to the inequity of desire
between you and me.

The Wait

time stands still
I linger
like the empty pitcher
at the mouth of the village well
waiting patiently

Absence

that night never left me,
it seeped into the hollow of my bones,
people leave—their absence doesn't,
it goes where the loss goes to hide.
inside the bones, in the hollow,
filling it with an immeasurable emptiness

Needs

Love waits at a street corner
where shadows hold the sunlight
remembering places
we had promised to visit
but never did
you were always busy
I was always living
our needs never coincided

Estrangement

last night we argued
you'd found my poems
about an imagined affair
we talked, I tried to reassure
but you disbelieved me
we slept in separate rooms

on the table at dawn
scattered breadcrumbs
unfinished coffee
and a few parting words
pinned to a page—
beautiful but dead

everything was perfect
in the life we shared
until familiarity and ego
cast their pall of silence
across this winter morning
veiled in mist and rain

I mourn the love that's lost
and struggle to accept
this end to all we had
imposed so ruthlessly on me—
two poems and a conversation
the cause of all my grief

TRAVEL

Solitude

I watched her from the tea shop
seated on the stone facing the valley
her back was to me, a joint in one hand
a cup of ginger lemon tea in the other
rings of smoke came from her lips,
their perfect seam tinged blue,
part of her turning to ash,
part of her drifting into the sky
the lengthening shadows of evening
held us in their stillness
as we watched our solitude
stark and sharply silhouetted
against the walls we built

Waiting

water dripped from the slate roof of the abandoned house
that perched at the crest of the ridge overlooking the valley,
rain clouds had raced to the distant mountain summits
leaving behind a landscape bejewelled with raindrops,
high above the valley, a double rainbow arched,
its ends lost among the autumnal foliage of the trees

a missed turn can lead you to unexpected places
and here I was beneath a canopy of dripping leaves,
in the backyard of nowhere, watching a dream unfold,
the sun, that had made a momentary appearance,
was now gone, obscured again by heavy clouds,
the rainbow was an apparition in the mist shrouded valley

a flock of birds swooped noisily into the trees for shelter,
one of nature's unerring harbingers of an impending storm,
from above the mist, the mountain silhouettes gazed down,
at the house, at me, ghosts, waiting, until everything crumbled.

Trail

the stone steps lead to a clearing
on the slope of the mountain
but today I'm taking an unknown trail,
shifting the weight of my backpack
I listen to the silence of the trees
as the leaves spiral down and dance
to imaginary music along the pathway,
they cling to my worn sneakers,
my gaze follows two pairs of wings
chasing each other in the clear, blue sky

I pause between Cedars and Oaks
taking in the rhythms of the landscape,
the path passes through the forest,
then dips, I hear the sound of water,
it makes the silence more apparent,
here, there is no such thing as time,
I inhale the hot fragrance of the day
and share my breath with you,
to you I may be only a memory,
to me, you are a pause in my thoughts

Echo

a window opens through time,
scented by Deodars and Pines,
as I lie on the balcony of our cottage,
my eyes linger on silhouettes
of Dhauladhars rising beyond the valley,
a breeze tugs at murmuring leaves,
forgetting to set, the sun filters
through swaying branches
and meanders along forgotten paths,
a twist of smoke rises to meet the sky,
I breathe deeply, eyes closed,
inhale the aromas we once shared,
the crackling warmth of a wood stove,
the tang of our salt-laced bodies,
their steam rising into the stillness
like the dreams haunting this house,
outside the time advances slowly

Kinnaur Revisited: a prose poem

The Himalayan foothills dwarf the bridge at Karcham, and stark winter light reveals the sculpted mountains, as I cross the roaring river and take the precipitous road to Kinnaur.
The town of Rampur Bushair fades away into a seemingly bottomless gorge, carved by the angry Sutlej it grinds through the deep gloom like a fearsome demon, rampaging along the edge of the mountain.
Guarded by the overhanging cliffs, the bridle path, follows the contours of hills which fade into a forest of tall pines cloaked in night, they stand meditating like the followers of an ancient cult to some forgotten God, the only sound comes from the blue-green Baspa, the trees drip icy green over its wintry cloud banks.
Night has invaded the valley, and in the chilly air I tremble for a familiar warmth. My memories of you lift me to the moon-swept hills that fall into the snow-haunted valleys, the silhouetted trees whisper the language of the wind, lonesome roads disappear in mist and rain, puddles on the white roads stare up like stranded mirrors.
Waylaid, the night snuggles into the bed of morning, wakes up ash-faced in a deserted alley of a city that has forgotten how to love or live.
I open my eyes, light a cigarette, somewhere time died in misty solitude and the river between us froze.

The German Bakery—Bhagsunag

Towering conifers support the starry sky
and, apart from a few mountain dogs,
barking loudly, the streets are deserted.
a few hours ago, the hills were alive,
awash with radiance; they rise now,
somnolent shadows against an ebony sky.

Like a *flaneur*, I amble through time
abandoned on the village pathways,
recalling when life could be measured
by faded blue jeans, chillam drags,
guitar strings, rum and disillusionment.
That was before we became lovers.

Laced with Old Monk and cinnamon,
the scented air of this summer night
lures me to the same German Bakery
where I once wrote long forgotten poems.
Inside the bakery, on our favourite table,
the chessboard, the chessmen still wait.

In the shadows, a group of foreigners
are being warmed by the kitchen fire.
In a tree nearby a fledgling screams,
startling birds roosting for the night
its cry swells and sinks into the valley,
as the moth-eaten moon watches silently.

Under the stars, night becomes still again;
the fiery liquid of the dark rum I ordered,
warms and soothes my dry, lovelorn tongue,
Then I shake my heart free of your dust
and walk to yet more familiar places—
places with the scents of other memories.

Rhanikhet

night shivers on quiet trees, the moon,
torn by the branches of conifers,
drags its light over the rustling deodars,
drops behind the houses at the valley's edge
the air smells of tobacco smoke and old wood
silence and regret haunts me
as I feel your absence growing like moss
on the walls of our abandoned home,
when shadows take shape, I think it is you
but you never come here now,
every night I wander among your memories,
hoping to feel your presence,
and when time rolls up the night
like an old prayer mat, and puts it away,
I return to my cold, silent grave
carrying the dust of our dreams

House

the shadow of the Oak trees
lies heavy on the grass below
no life stirs in the green expanse
that stretches until it meets the sky
with its cargo of clouds

along the distant ridge of hills
dust rises from a winding road
that looks lazily down
upon the slowly moving river
that crosses the land

along that road is our house
the house we loved and shared
until the day we drifted apart
now that lonely house waits
hoping again to become a home

Wait

I often walk on lonely trails
sometimes the jungle mist
drifts like a sad song
sometimes it rains

my only companions then
are the silence inside me
and the longing in my heart
for all that could not be ours

when I face the mountains
I look far into the valley
where a house rests quietly
beneath the dhauladhars

it waits for you there
when evening comes
the dying light of the sun
illuminates the snow peaks

like prayer lamps in a window
and I imagine your silhouette
with the breeze gently weaving
sunlight through your hair

I have often walked these trails
but none have led me to you
so here I sit, staring at the house
at the mountain peaks, at the valley

from where you will soon appear
in my reverie I wait for you—
your bag filled with dreams
and the sun in your hand

Drought

sun pounds on cracked slate roofs
razor edged shadows cut the streets
a zephyr moans in empty spaces
scorching everywhere it goes

as I walk through this dying town
once a thriving place—and watch
aged paint curl on crumbling walls
as melting asphalt binds my shoes

a quiet lane takes me through time
the world was green—full of food
then children laughed so happily
long before this drought began

now all around is grit and dust
trees bleached white—dry as bones
shadows deepen on scorched walls
I lose myself in their dark stains

trying to soothe my weary mind
I follow the river baked with heat
to leave the town where I belonged
knowing tonight I'll dream of rain

On the Banks of the Ganges

time stands still
on the stone steps by the river;
a silhouette takes a dip
and emerges from the waters,
hands folded
in obeisance to the rising sun,
a brief transition
from the mundane to the divine.

A marigold garland
drifts by with ash in a plastic bag,
with a conch's cry,
the temple city quivers to life,
a flower boy approaches
with a frail female form in white,
a prayer basket
trembling in her parchment hands.

She faces the river,
obliviously chants her mantras,
lights the flower lamp,
sets it afloat on the sluggish water
a song comes
as a boatman begins his day's work
the sun rises
lifting the veil from Shiva's abode.

The air thickens
around the saffron tinted waters,
smoke rises
from funeral pyres and cooking fires,
their backdrop
a skyline of soot-darkened temples,
In this sacred city—
Varanasi a place of human contrasts—

suffering and liberty,
birth, death and so many sacred rituals,
the awakening of life
as I walk the ghats they come alive,
with rhythmic sounds
as washer men thrash their laundry
against stone slabs,
a holy man—his body smeared with ash—

lifts his hands
above his head in prayer, while another,
with dreadlocks,
is deep in meditation at the sunken temple,
the air echoes
with the clanging sound of temple bells,
pigeons take flight,
from under a canopy I watch the Ganges
gasp for breath
at this confluence of life and death.

Ruins

under a melancholy sky
drenched in blood,
the ecstasy of love
and the anguish of loneliness,
bleed over the canyons
of light and shadow
rising from the grey stones,

stairs leading nowhere,
narrow pathways, aging walls
transfixed in pain, dimly alive,
dusk settling into their cracks—
looted, betrayed, traded
in this labyrinth of solitude
decayed by the passing of time,
I still linger unperceived,
not knowing where to go,
or where to return to,
my weight of memories
is heavier that those
blocks of orphaned stone,
the all-embracing night

descends like a great shadow
onto our shared loneliness,
flowing into our crevices,
filling the emptiness, the void,

making everything like itself,
surpassing the idle details,
singing a requiem for the living.

The Last Meal

we were together but alone
the distance between us
like the table at the dhaba
where we often stopped
en-route to the mountains
we sat opposite each other
breathing in the aromas
from the open kitchen
an old man sitting nearby
began to hum a melody
a familiar tune that carried me
to places I longed to see with you—
those Himalayan villages
with quaint, slate-roofed houses
those hidden waterfalls
the colourful prayer flags
the distant moon and stars—
the old man fall silent
rising spice trails
from the sizzling pans
end my reverie, I smile
as you pick at *khubz tandoor*
taking time to savour
the hunter's moon
dripping through your fingers

*Khubz tandoor–flatbread made in tandoor (clay oven)

MOSAIC

Empty Is Full

deserted corridors are not empty,
they are full of whatever you imagine
in the quietness of silence
between dark shadows and light
like an ancient dream
lingers a phantasm
waiting to be discovered

Poetry This Month is Hexed

I am hunting for words,
in the marginalia
and in the frail silences
that crumble at my touch.
My mouth is filled with the
warm metallic taste of loss,
I bleed in letters of a language
I no longer understand

Every day a fresh page—
smudged words, dead paragraphs,
images, music and sketches
skirmishes, idiosyncrasies,
noises and distractions,
visual ideas, blotches of ink.

There is a storm in my fingertips.
"Don't write of angst," I'm told,
but I don't want to wear a mask
I want to lay myself bare
I want you to see how
your love has affected me..

Lost Poems

on my mind are some poems long forgotten
pressed between the pages of an old book
poems written in a language i no longer know
poems carrying the scent of some other time
or some other place, now just a shadow
on this sultry summer afternoon i sit back
with a glass of mint infused lemonade
and think of these decaying autumn leaves
which once were fresh, tender and green

Daydream

The street is sultry, shaded by a curtain of light,
the mysterious green of motionless leaves,
in between fronds are plumes of cinder red sky.

The air, motionless but for a nascent breeze,
heavy with the smell and heat of fresh macadam,
is filled with the constant sound of unseen feet.

I sit in my own quiet place, a private haven,
shape shifting, changing colours as I float
among wondrous hues borrowed from dreams.

I am visible, not visible, present, absent, existing,
not existing; thoughts merge, ideas coincide—
despite me, the universe continues to evolve.

In my shifting reality I seem to lose all control,
just as the poet does, who creates, who writes,
and who disappears into the morass of words.

Illusions

I read, I read and I read
until nothing is left to read—
except the newspapers—
then I take to the windows

I begin to fill my empty hours
by gazing deeply into time
that seldom seems to move
on either side of the frame

my wall calendar changes
seasons change, people change
but the stillness remains
my inner silence remains

untouched… unchanging
at night, my walls are a presence
they change, I feel them feel
and then they are walls again

just an expanse of solid black
enclosing me, until the light
that always hides at the edges
comes swiftly to end my illusions

Melancholia is...

a language
that is beyond words
that breathes and festers
behind the shadows of time

a language…
that lingers as a nightmare
beneath the waking mind
creating unseen turmoil

a language…
of ancient hills, weary roads
winter nights and snowfall,
of distant shorelines

a language…
a dissonance, dark, endearing
in the moaning of the rocks,
and the cries from the stars

a longing for…
a poem gone astray
a reflective footnote
a haunting noctuary

the sound of…
footsteps on narrow stairs
in draughty corridors
and a funeral in the rain

hopelessness…
a shadow of despair
a feeling for dark days
loneliness and sorrow

melancholia is…
as low as life becomes
before darkness ends
and sunrise brings hope

Troubled Seasons

I escaped the autumn of her womb,
became part of an eternal winter,
the broken shards of summer
still trapped within my throat,
the rain, imprisoned by time,
simmered in dark hollows,
silently I shed my skin again,
the autumn I hoped to escape
still a torrent in my veins
that branched like a river
across a disturbed landscape
nibbling the invisible dark,
there is no escape here
from what thrives and festers deep—
discarded shadows seeking vengeance

Scent

he'd crossed a continent
to be with her at last;
overwhelmed by his scent,
she reaches for him
and draws him close,
her full nippled breasts
brushing against his chest,
they hold each other close,
then their lips meet—
through the bar windows
streams soft afternoon light

in their virtual assignations,
they had merged their beings
for months—apart yet together,
now close at last, they talk,
they laugh, they tenderly kiss,
as their romance becomes real,
one day, this time will end
only nostalgia will remain,
memories of moments shared
in nondescript bars and hotels,
and a question—was it real?

Exhaustion—1

half enshrouded, a quarter moon—
a slice of pizza Margherita,
stars, buttered popcorn

wrapped in the soundless dark,
on an anaesthetic night,
I lie on a bench in an empty park

head in the crook of my left arm,
a half burnt cigarette loosely held
by two fingers of my right hand

a mangy dog approaches, hesitating,
cautious, sniffs at my muddy shoes,
thinks better of it and retreats

my shoes smell of death and decay,
of hunger, thirst, sweat and blood,
of drudgery, sleeplessness and pain

my eyes stare into the darkness,
a breeze rustles through the trees,
leaves speak, but I don't understand

my cigarette turns to ash, it falls,
night gathers the leftovers, distant now
the dog howls a lullaby for the hungry

Exhaustion—2

Each day she sets out to work
before dawn's first light,
each day she returns home
through the gathering darkness,
always she has a single thought—
who will be fed that night,
and who will suffer hunger.

Her life, a struggle to feed mouths,
for that's all her family is to her,
means she slaves for their existence,
her limbs always aching, exhausted,
her life of no more consequence,
just like her dreams, her desires,
her grief and unending despair.

Weighed down by her sense of duty
she leans tiredly against a tree,
she gazes at the darkening plains,
her desperate eyes limp and leaden;
she is enslaved by the cycle of labour,
no, not labour—vicious drudgery,
that is hopeless, endless, joyless.

She folds her hands in supplication,
asks forgiveness for a final act
she is determined to carry out.
Silhouetted against the near dark sky

against the stars, a darker darkness,
slowly turning, swaying, fading—
earth to earth, ashes to ashes, dust to dust.

Exhaustion—3

The poet is a hungry spirit,
always at the peak of stimulation
and the nadir of total exhaustion,
from daybreak to nightfall to daybreak,
always searching for equilibrium.

Break-Up

as you slammed that door on me
the slats of the shutters
cut my shadow into strips
I stood there
on the sunlit sidewalk
my fragmented self
suddenly coherent

Pause

A winterized spring
summer still waiting at the threshold.
Who has cast the spell on the seasons?
If it was not for the Autumn within me
there would be no poems.

Nocturne

night rain,
just the quiet slithering,
the smell of thunder,
tree shadows
disappearing in darkness
and a neon moon
illuminating a puddle.

ACROSTICS

Journey

January, a night, grim and desolate
on a lonely, moonlit highway
unfurling quietly, frostily still,
rugged mountains scratching the dark,
nocturnal creatures calling the moon,
even the leafless trees whisper,
yesterday is gone, tomorrow is asleep

Silhouette

solitary against the evening sky,
in a land no longer hers, she stands
leaning against an ancient tree,
haunting–like a shadow of herself,
overhead the branches braid the sky,
uncanny limbs laid bare and stark
empty of all offerings
time stands still–as does her heart,
the sun has died a crimson death
easing her transition into night

River-Song

reverberating with echoes of the past
iridescent against the silver of the sky
veering west along the fringes of the forests
embracing the contours of stony outcrops
roll the haunted waters in a deepening gloom
singing a requiem for things that are lost
of the people who are now no more
nestled at its bank sorrow grieves
growing green with the slightest rain

Phantasm

poised between the unknown and the known
hidden in the depth of night's shadows
an ancient dream lingers barely alive
nebulous, an ethereal remnant of desire
tangled in the endless skeins of time
a spectre of so many memories
sorrow fills my heart as I see it fade
merging effortlessly into the morning light

Topography

That mole in the hollow of your back is a secret place
obscure until my tongue traces your spine's trajectory
painting an intimate landscape, vast and varied
often the feral scent of sex clings to my skin
growing as you move to uncharted places
reclaiming territories old and new
and spaces filled with the weight of love
pressed together our bodies are a terra incognita where
heat lines radiate like the contours of the earth
your mole a primeval star leading me homewards

Funeral Pyre

fire licked corpses are the first thing you witness,
upstream the hot air carries the stench of death,
near the foul water mixing with the black ash
each body, covered in brightly spangled shrouds,
rests on a bier before being taken to a pyre
alongside the ghats that lead down to the river,
looking peaceful, but tainted with misery and sin,
pyres blaze, smoke rises, flames flash sunwards
you hear the cracking of bones, the crackle of logs
recently you were consumed in that searing heat
eyes closed dreaming, melting, floating, yielding

*Ghats – stone steps that lead to the holy river Ganges in Benares

DELHI POEMS

Hazrat Nizamuddin Auliya Dargah

Love and faith light up the tangle of streets
that lead to the dargah of mehbub-e-ilahi,
and the tomb of his beloved disciple Khusro,
garbed in rose petals, attars, offerings
and with a heady whiff of spiced kebabs.
Lost words float across the treetops,
arches, patios and tombs, sometimes,
quietly, they curl in an empty nest
or whirl down onto the marbled floor
in an aerial dance—like dervishes,
caught in a mystical ecstasy, their souls
electrified by the crescendo of qawwals.

Possessed in a feverish frenzy of longing
and sensuousness, bodies merge
and become the saint and the poet,
love rises, as smoke at the end of incense
and floats through the prayers
tied to the marble lattice.
I sit in a corner, eyes closed—entranced,
the poet in me loses herself to the scents,
the sounds, the sights, the dust, the birds,
the trees, the sky, the marble, the songs,
and then dips herself in holy water
as green as the greenest emerald.

The sun seeks its path among
the silhouettes frozen in time.

I lean on the afternoon draped pillars
and feel my inner darkness melt
into their lengthening shadows,
the ancient walls soak up the pain
as my finger's trace time's erosion.
Across the courtyard, time, like a poem,
burns in the dua-e-roshni as the day
meets the loban perfumed night.
Two lovers completing each other
like reunited hemispheres.

It is this cosmos wherein exists
the inexpressible, visible only
to those with eyes which can see.

[1]. Hazrat Nizamuddin Auliya Dargah is the mausoleum of one of the famous Sufi saints Hazrat Kwaja Nizamuddin Auliya (1238-1325 CE). One of Delhi's best mystical and magical cultural experiences, this shrine is visited by hundreds of devotees and music lovers every day.
[2]. Mehbub-e-ilahi – Beloved of God.
[3]. Khusro – Hazrat Amir Khusro, an outstanding poet, scholar and musician, was Hazrat Nizamuddin Auliya's favourite disciple. Khusro's tomb is part of the Nizamuddin dargah complex.
[4]. Qawwals – Qawwali is a form of Sufi devotional music derived from the word Qawl (utterance) and Qawwals are the singers who perform the qawwali.
[5]. Dua e roshni – prayer of light is recited in the evening (when the day meets the night) by the Khadims (attendents) of the dargah. That time of the day is considered auspicious to seek the blessings from the saint. This daily ritual is centuries old and the prayer is said after lighting the lamps which is an exclusive privilege of the dargah khadims.
[6]. Loban – Frankincense – a resinous incense burned during ceremonies and prayers.

Lodi Garden

The fringes of the day lingered
on the ramparts of Lodi's tomb,
flowed onto the octagonal walls
and their tall arches and columns
that stood like trees of life
recalling that glorious past.
Sunlight played hide and seek
on the buildings as it sought its path
among silhouettes frozen in time.

I took a path shaded by arching trees,
the earlier crowds had thinned,
and love was all around—on the rocks,
behind trees, on the eight-pier bridge,
on the steps of ancient mausoleums,
in quiet corners screened by bamboos,
it even sprawled on the sloppy lawns
unconcerned by the scattered graves,
or the cacophonous roosting birds.

Love doesn't care about the mundane,
nor does dust from the ancient bones
of the dynasties that shaped Delhi.
I passed happy, laughing children
as they teased ducks by the pond,
in the shade of a flowering Kachnar
and then sat, eyes squinting in the light,
a blade of grass between my teeth,
watching the never quite empty sky.

The shadows of leaves stirred
as a breeze blew through the trees,
a pair of cooing doves paused to listen
to the rustling whispers around them,
from the parapets, dark birds flew
like fragments of charred paper
rising from a flourishing fire.
A kite watched from a lonely turret,
hoping for prey in the afternoon sun.

Leaving the comfort of shadow play
I took the familiar path back to reality
harsh headlights, noise, groping hands,
streets filled with catcalls and swearing,
dust and fumes choking the city's lungs,
green grass merging into concrete,
and night, now creeping across the sky
hiding the many sins of a crowded city
more ruinous than the ruins I left behind.

Lodi – Sikander Lodi was the second ruler of Lodi dynasty who reigned in Delhi from 1489-1517CE)

Purple Rain: a prose poem

There was a time when the wide avenues of Lutyen's Delhi exploded with purple prose.
Walking from Ashoka Road, traversing India gate and going to Rajpath, on languid, monsoon afternoons, one could watch the sweet, earthy notes colouring the city's tongue violet.
Chasing the thieving parakeets, children foraged for the dark cousin of grapes. The explosion of flavours puckered their mouths—a bit of Indian summer right there.
As I walk along the purple strewn memory lane, a little head pops out from under an umbrella tilted on the sidewalk, "Jamun?" its voice asks. A palm, stained like an artist's palette offers a few glistening fruits. Tempted, I bite into one, bitter-sweet and astringent all at once, memories of you explode in my mouth.
Inked by the only city I know, I walk along the leafy avenue drenched in purple rain. One of many rains I try to catch on my tongue.

Medical Migrants

Outside Delhi's one-hundred acre
'premier' hospital complex,
the road, perpetually struggles to breathe,
by the hospital gates, under a plastic sheet,
so does the man whose wife and children
huddle by a makeshift stove for warmth.

Nearby, beneath a tattered blanket,
a woman moans, she is only half awake,
the acrid fumes of tarmac burn her eyes.
Oblivious to the cold, dust and fumes
hordes of poor medical migrants
bide their time under the harsh sky.

Waiting, sometimes for months or years,
clutching their belongings and medical files
they spill onto the surrounding lanes,
the bus stands and the Metro Station.
Within a five kilometre radius of the hospital,
a flourishing parallel economy thrives.

It caters to the needs of those who wait,
men, women, children, old and young.
Food stalls, pharmacists, path-labs,
photocopying bureaus, beggars, hawkers
and even a temple, all make a living
by relieving the poor of what they have

In the parking lot, among the parked cars,
a dusty black hearse is conspicuous
by its shimmering golden streamers,
it waits, knowing business will come.
In this city everyone can benefit
from the endless trade in life and death.

Scent of a Season

sitting on the veranda at dusk
I count the curling leaves on a tree,
as I feel autumn in my bones

a lemon-scented breeze…
memories, in my hands, crumbling,
clusters of Saptparni blooms.

their scent rising from pavements
white carpeted with fallen petals,
intoxicating the night above them

a smell of winter—nostalgia—
childhood, adolescence, youth, love,
late night cigarette sessions,
makeshift fires on the terrace,
Old Monk, spliffs, long drives,
and your breath against mine

in thinking of Lutyen's Delhi
there is more to it that lingers on
memories of a time I can't forget.

Summer, Noon in Delhi: a prose poem

On a humid summer noonday, from the confines of my twenty degrees Celsius air-conditioned life, I watch moving furnaces travel along the roads.
A Jacaranda has burst into purple prose below my window, the neighbour's Gulmohar tree paints vermilion graffiti across the ice blue sky.
The rickshaw puller hauls more than the weight he should for what he will be paid. His dreams of making it big in the city have evaporated as dreams do.
Running down his shoulders, they drip, and rise mirage-like from the asphalt, while the fiery sun owes no mercy as, relentlessly, it burns the skin from his back.
Swathed in grime and sweat, destined to atone for their sins under the surveillance of a cruel and barren sky, the street dwellers wilt, gasp and die.
From its dry fountain perch, a crow watches an exhausted dog slide beneath a parked car, seeking the solace of shade, its mouth dry as dust.
A sound signals a power cut. Inside the four walls, the temperature rises, the inverter brings a fan to life, and in the shadows of its turning blades my poem forms.

Fever

My body burns like a city set ablaze,
the touch of the air feels like a shrapnel,
my throat is a desert in storm.

Inside, thorns create a parallel language,
no flower blooms here, a relief,
I loathe lovers who betray.

In the opium haze mountains fade,
then emerge like my breath,
slowly rising, then falling.

The mind begins to shut down
as the heart curls between two notes
of a song long forgotten.

My tongue ambles in the streets of Delhi,
in the midst of this,
streets filled with the aromas of Eid.

In another town, my second born
celebrates his birthday,
the thought of him keeps me going.

The Lake

the dying rays of the day's sun
ripple over the darkening waters
as evening descends on the lake

your memory—a mirage of mist
rises from the mournful waters
under a lattice of bare branches

a breeze breaks the stillness
leaves rustle, the birds go silent
as they return to their nests

cicadas sing their song to night
as I wait for the moon to rise
the forest is a landscape of dreams

scents from the past come to me
as the stars slowly begin to fade
pale ghosts walk between the trees

they disappear into my thoughts
as I meander through my solitude
seeking something no longer there

the lake calls me to its depths
I float as a boat adrift in fog
bound for nowhere I can recall

Black and White

unquiet mind, quiet words
night is at the edge of my bed
as a whirling mass of black
arousing spectres from my past
possessed, I lie in quiet melancholy
until the sun explodes in my room
separating the night from dark
naked, I wait somewhere between
a lighter shade of white
and a darker shade of black

www.ingramcontent.com/pod-product-compliance
Lightning Source LLC
LaVergne TN
LVHW090116080426
835507LV00040B/935